Index

How to use this book

When first faced with piped borders they can appear overwhelming, the aim of *Border Inspirations* is to demystify them a little whilst providing a step by step guide. The magic number for this book is five; you will need a maximum of five nozzles to pipe every border in this book, some may take even less. On each page you will be faced with easy to follow steps to create a finished border (any piping shown in tan royal icing demonstrates the next step). Some borders will require the full five steps, whereas the simpler borders will not.

Where I have felt that added design elements could further enhance a piped border I have added sugar embellishments. These are suggestions to spark your own imagination and creativity, the creation of these simple elements will be covered in future publications.

What will I need?

- Bowl of royal icing
- Spatula
- Pallet knife
- Paper piping bags or plastic piping bags with a nozzle adaptor
- 5 nozzles – I have used PME Supatubes nos. 13, 44, 3, 2, 1 (other nozzles of a similar size are available from Wilton or other manufacturers)
- Small paintbrush (used to tidy up any peaks of royal icing during piping)
- Damp tea towel (to cover your bowl of royal icing)

Helpful hint

The designs in this book were piped right handed, however if you are left handed you will find them easier to pipe in the reverse direction. To see what these will look like view them in a mirror resting along the left hand side of the page.

The basics

Royal icing basics

When working with this versatile medium the making of royal icing is normally a cake decorator's first stumbling block. Once you have made it a couple of times you will wonder why you ever had a problem, like everything once you've got it, you've got it. If you have not made royal icing before, I have recorded a video on YouTube called *Making Royal Icing* which can be accessed through my website www.cerigriffiths.com.

Always ensure all the equipment you use to weigh, make, handle, pipe and store the royal icing is thoroughly washed in hot soapy water to remove any traces of grease. Grease is an enemy to royal icing and will destroy it, making it unusable.

I use a stand mixer. As a guide, if your machine comes with a dough hook for the making of bread or bun dough then it will be strong enough to make royal icing. If you only need a small amount of royal icing, for example a batch of 500g or less, then there are premix products readily available. Always thoroughly sieve pre-mixes prior to using them to evenly distribute the ingredients, this will guarantee a uniform consistency when beaten up. For larger batches I use the recipe shown or multiples of it depending on my requirements.

Ceri's royal icing recipe

This recipe uses real pasteurised egg whites so do not keep this royal icing for more than 4 days in its wet state. Once it is has dried, royal icing is edible for months as long as it is kept dust and damp-free.

Recipe:

60g Real pasteurised egg whites

2 Teaspoons of lemon juice

500g Icing or confectioners' sugar

Method:

Make sure all of your equipment has been washed in hot soapy water to ensure it is grease-free.

1. Crack your eggs and divide the yolk from the whites, make sure none of the yolk gets into the egg whites because egg yolk contains fat. Measure 60g of the egg whites into your mixing bowl.
2. Add the two teaspoons of lemon juice directly to the egg whites; this lemon juice could be from a bottle or a real lemon (with no bits).
3. Using a beater or paddle turn your machine onto a low speed for about one minute to break up the egg whites and lemon juice.
4. Weigh 500g of sieved icing or confectioners' sugar and add all of it to the egg whites and lemon juice in the mixing bowl.
5. Turn your machine onto its lowest setting, if you mix the royal icing too quickly it will incorporate too much air.
6. After one minute stop the machine and scrape down the inside of the machine bowl making sure that all ingredients are being incorporated.
7. Turn your machine back on to the slow speed and mix for another two minutes, and then once again scrape the bowl down.
8. After mixing your royal icing for a further one minute it should be ready to use. At this point should you want a softer eating royal icing for coating your cakes then I would recommend adding 2 teaspoons of glycerine at this stage. Do not add glycerine if you are planning to pipe flowers or do any fine piping such as line work, off-pieces or extension work.

Storing royal icing

1. When you have finished working with your bowl of royal icing at the end of the day, scrape the sides of the bowl down, smoothing the royal icing to a flat surface.
2. Using a clean, damp cloth wipe the insides of the bowl. If there is any icing on the sides of the bowl, and it crusts then drops into your royal icing, you will have lumps which will cause you problems and block piping nozzles.
3. Place a piece of plastic wrap directly over the surface of the royal icing. This should actually be in contact with the surface of the royal icing. Try to make sure there are no air pockets, and that the plastic wrap is also in contact with the inside surfaces of the bowl.
4. Lay a damp clean tea towel over the top of the bowl and set aside.
5. When you come to use royal icing after storage you do not need to remix it in a machine. Giving it a beat by hand using a spatula will be enough to re-establish the consistency of the royal icing.
6. I personally do not keep my royal icing for more than four days, as the royal icing tends to start breaking down in strength and structure and should only be used for coating and not piping.
7. I do not normally store my royal icing in the refrigerator; room temperature is the normal for storing royal icing, however in the height of summer I will put my royal icing bowl in the fridge overnight if necessary. It is important to note that if your royal icing has been in the fridge, you should let it reach room temperature again before re-beating it by hand and using.

Consistencies

Firm peak

When you lift your pallet knife away from the surface of the royal icing it will form a spike or peak which will hold its form.

Soft peak

When you lift your pallet knife away from the surface of the royal icing it will form a spike or peak which will curl over at its tip.

Run out

This is firm peak royal icing which has had extra reconstituted Meri-White or egg white stirred into it. Run out icing should be a thick pourable consistency similar to thick honey or treacle. As a rough guide if you drizzle some of the run out icing onto its own surface it should take a slow count of eight for it to blend back into itself. It is important to note that run out icing should be stirred and left to stand for a while to allow any bubbles to rise to the surface prior to use.

Firm peak

Soft peak

Run out

Paper piping bag

When piping borders they are normally piped using a larger plastic or nylon piping bag fitted with a coupler, however I have found that when piping line work or finer detailed elements then a parchment piping bag gives me more dexterity and control.

1. A piping bag is normally made from a triangle of one of the following types of paper: Parchment, Greaseproof or Silicone, the choice is a personal preference. When you purchase your chosen paper you will either buy a roll of paper or sheets, both of which you will have to cut into triangles. Some sugarcraft shops do sell pre-cut triangles.

2. Choose one of the top corners and turn it over to meet the bottom point of your triangle; this will give you a basic cone shape. Now select the remaining top corner and wrap it around the cone so that both of the corners and the point roughly line up, don't worry about them meeting at this point.

3. By holding the base of your piping bag in both hands you should be able to slide the layers of paper in and out of the cone until the top of the cone becomes a sharp point. It is important to get the point of your cone as sharp as possible because if it is loose it will unwind when you start to pipe.

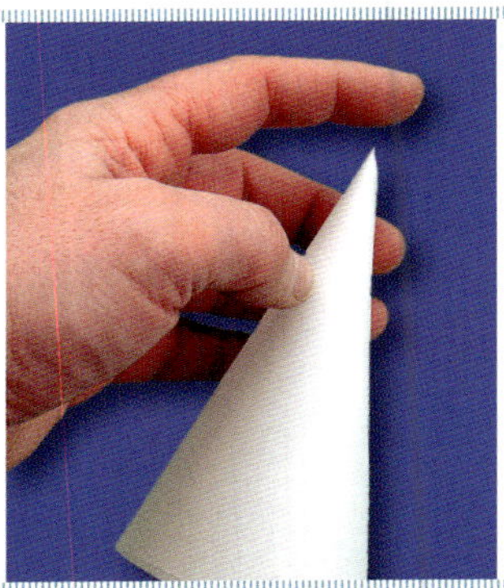

4. When you have a sharp point to your cone there are two methods for aligning the different layers of paper at the base of your piping bag. Some decorators will line all of the ends up to create one single point; some decorators will overlap them to create an M shape, as shown here. If you create the M shape you will have overlapping layers of paper which will strengthen the piping bag at its weakest point, which is the seam.

5. To complete the piping bag, fold over the points at the base, and then fold them over again. This will give you the style of piping bag you would normally get if you were to purchase pre-made piping bags.

6. Using a pair of scissors make two small cuts in the folded paper making sure not to cut more than half the width of the folded paper. Fold over the cut tab of paper, this will help lock the layers of paper in place and should help prevent the bag from coming unwound when you fill it. No guarantees though.

7. I normally get asked "How much do I cut off my piping bag for my piping tip?" As a rule you should never cut more than half of the overall length of your piping tip off the end of your piping bag. If a measurement helps I would suggest cutting off approx 1cm from the end of the piping bag for your piping tip.

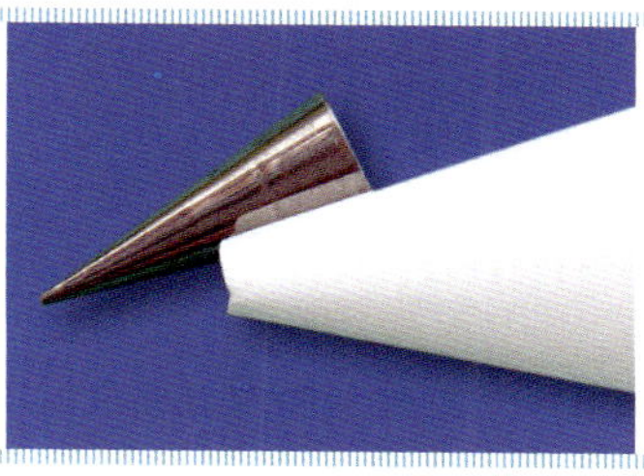

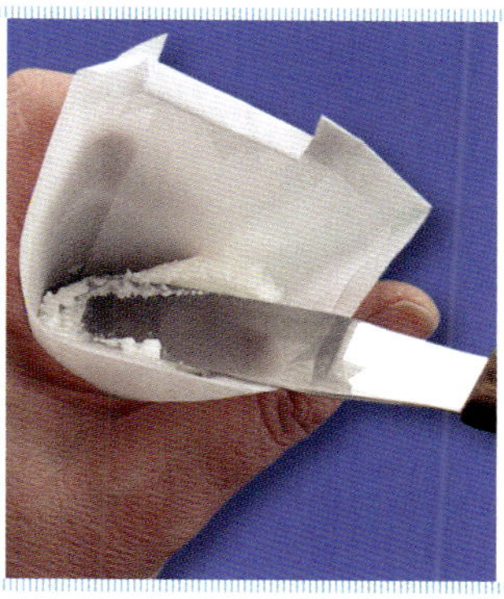

8. When filling the piping bag decorators are normally too timid, if you aim to only half fill your bag and do it with conviction you should be fine. Put only enough icing onto your palette knife that will fit into the opening in your piping bag, insert the palette knife and then press the flat blade down firmly onto the side of your thumb and gently slide your palette knife out wiping the icing off the blade and into the bag. This method normally means you don't pull the centre of the bag out when you remove the palette knife.

9. Now close the bag and press the icing down towards the piping tip, fold the top over twice towards you making sure that the seam of the bag is furthest away from you.

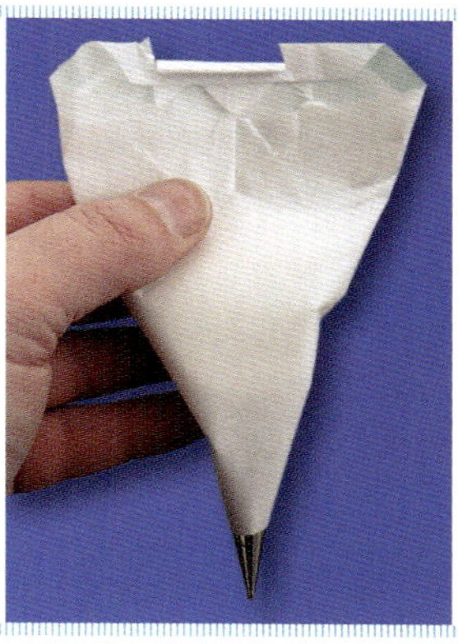

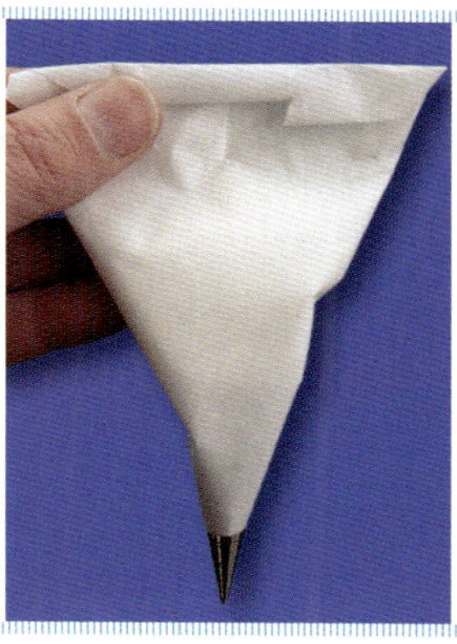

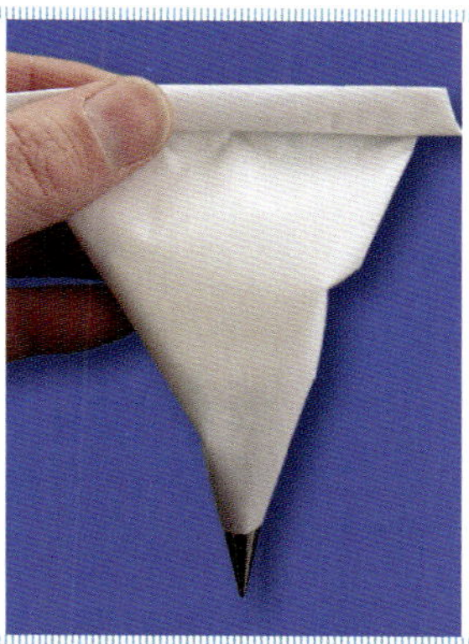

10. Fold the corners of the bag into the centre and then give it one more fold towards the piping tip. I know this sounds like a lot of folding but this method means that it is very unlikely that your icing will come out of the wrong end of the bag whilst you are piping, it also gives you a good fold of paper to press against.

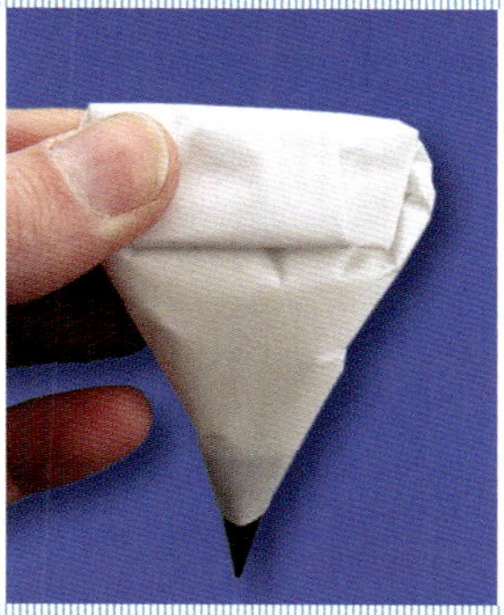

11. You now have a piping bag filled and ready to use. I cannot stress enough that you need to fold away from the seam when you fold the filled piping bag as this will tighten the seam, fold towards the seam and it will gape and weaken the piping bag at the tip.

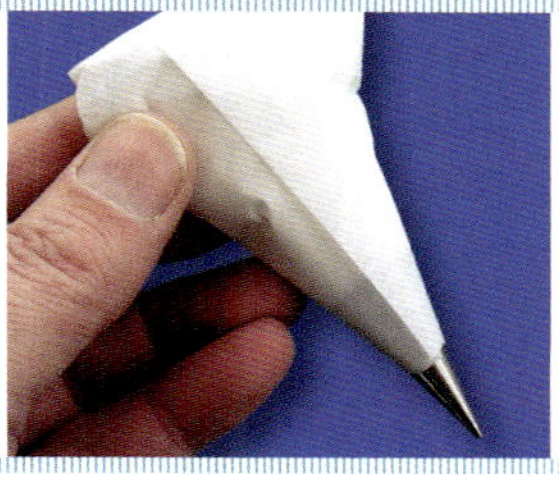

Border basics

Piped borders have a language and as with any language there is an alphabet, luckily there are only two letters in this alphabet so it is easily learnt. The letters are S and C; the majority of piped borders are a combination of these two letters and commonly referred to by these same letters re: S scroll, Double S scroll, S and C scroll, S and reverse C scroll, etc. If you look closely at any piped border it is more than likely created from a combination of these two letters as they can be piped in any direction and are sometimes elongated or distorted in some way. You will occasionally come across a drape or a scoop in a border, so if you view these as a C without the curl at its end then you won't go far wrong. If you look at the sections of a scroll you will find it is only a shaped rope with a tail. The skill is in the amount of pressure used to achieve the overall shape. The foundations beneath a royal iced border can take different forms, however the most common are the Rope, Barrel or Shell; examples of each of these are shown. You will often find in the more complex piped borders a combination of these are used.

When referring to 'line work' this is the piping of lines of icing on top of each other, or by the side of each other, in decreasing sized nozzles, e.g. 3, 2, 1 (then a no. 0 if piping a top line in colour).

For line work on the top of a border use this guide:

1
2
3
Top of piped border

For line work on top of a cake on the inside edge of a border use this guide:

Inside edge of border on top of cake	1		
	2	1	
	3	2	1

For line work on the side of a cake beneath a barrel use this guide:

On the side of a cake beneath a barrel	3	2	1
	2	1	
	1		

A piped border should be viewed as a picture frame to your cake; it should enhance your creation and gently bring the eye to the centrepiece, inscription, motif etc. A word of warning, an overly ornate piped border on a cake which is too small to carry it will make your cake look heavy and dated.

When designing a cake with piped borders always bear in mind that the borders should be size appropriate, adding to the overall impact of the cake and not distracting from it. Also be aware that the public's preconceived view of a cake with large amounts of royal icing piped work is that it is dated and old fashioned, so be clever at the design stage and contemporary with your use of royal icing.

Piping skills are a wonderful way to add the wow factor to your cake designs with the only limitation being your imagination. Cake artists and Sugarcrafters alike are constantly coming up with new ways to enhance their work by pushing the boundaries of royal icing, so don't be afraid to experiment with this versatile medium.

If you have not piped borders before, I have recorded a video on YouTube called *'Border Basics for Royal Icing'* which can be accessed through my website www.cerigriffiths.com.

Step by step

Initial border shapes

A basic shell border piped with a no. 13 star nozzle. A shell can be piped with any round tipped nozzle of any size, plain or star, dependent on your finished design.

A basic rope border piped with a no. 13 star nozzle. A rope can be piped with any round tipped nozzle of any size, plain or star, dependent on your finished design.

A barrel piped with a no. 13 star nozzle. A barrel can be piped with any round tipped nozzle of any size, plain or star, dependent on your finished design. For scroll work the nozzles used would be traditionally a no. 13 or a no. 44.

The image on the left is the basic shape of an S scroll and a guide for piping, whilst the image on the right is an S Scroll piped with a no. 44 nozzle.

The image on the left is the basic shape of a C scroll and a guide for piping, whilst the image on the right is a C Scroll piped with a no. 44 nozzle.

Spirals

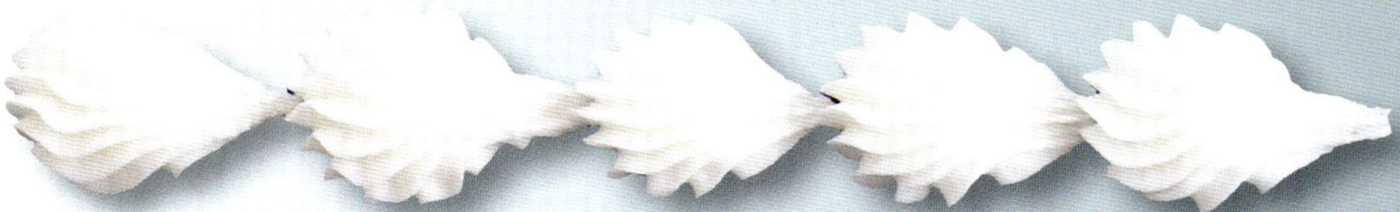

Step 1 Pipe large shells using a no. 13 nozzle.

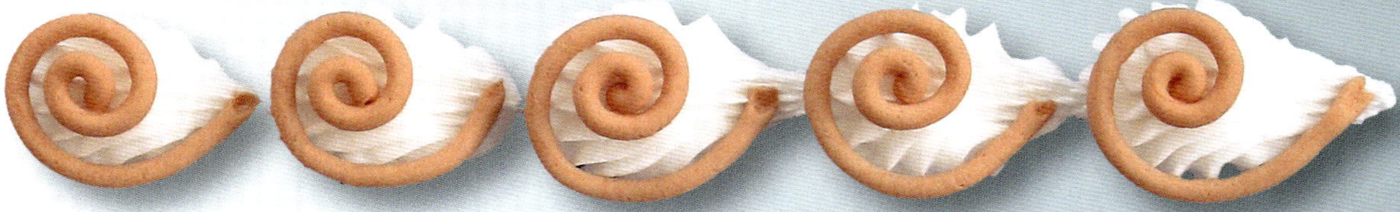

Step 2 Pipe line work in a spiral fashion stacking the lines on top of each other using nozzle nos. 3, 2, 1.

Step 3 This is how your border will appear once complete.

Step 4 The addition of a small autumn leaf will give this border a masculine feel.

Step 5 The addition of a small rose will give the same border a more feminine touch.

Ceri's comments

"A neat border which will work for any shaped cake and suits either the top or bottom edges. When you pipe the shells it is important to leave more of a gap than usual between the tail of a shell and the head of the next one if you wish to add any decorative elements, as shown here."

Lazy hearts

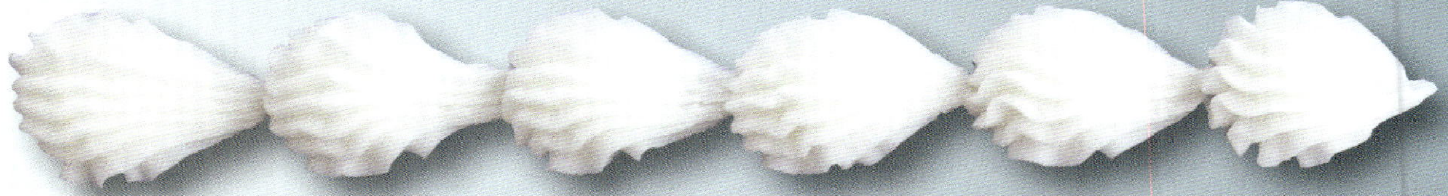

Step 1 Pipe shells using a no. 13 nozzle.

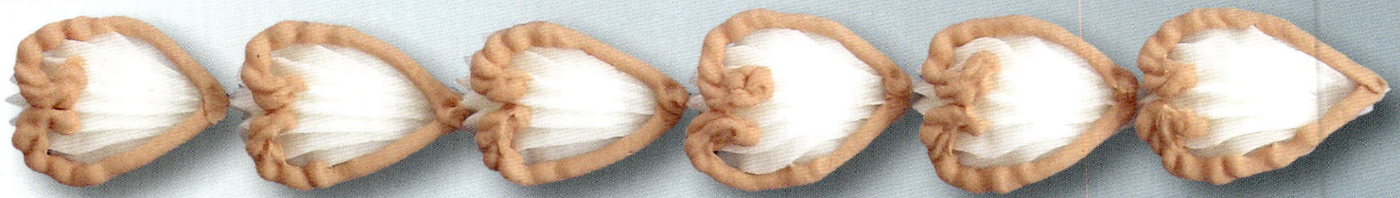

Step 2 Pipe a pair of small mirrored C scrolls with a no. 3 nozzle to establish the heart shape.

Step 3 Over-pipe the C scrolls using a no. 3 nozzle, staying in contact with the scroll beneath as this will establish a smooth base for your line work.

Step 4 Pipe line work stacking the lines on top of each other using nozzle nos. 3, 2, 1.

Step 5 This is a clean very simple border which is perfect for the romantic at heart.

Ceri's comments

"A simple yet impressive border if piped well. When piping make sure that your shells are not too close together as this will cause you problems when you pipe the heart shapes. This border works best for a top border but if used as a bottom border expect the heart motif to be more compressed."

Shell and blade

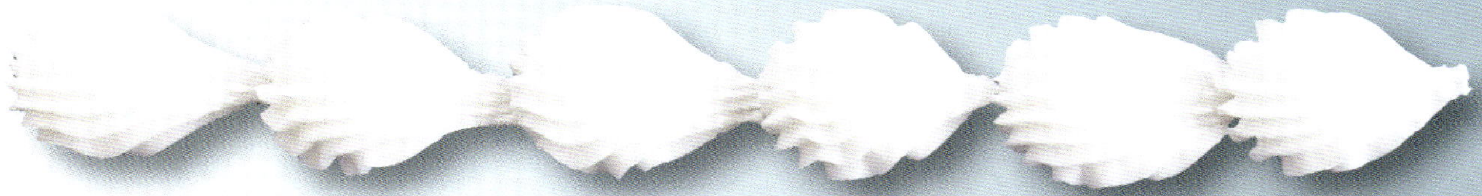

Step 1 Pipe large shells using a no. 13 nozzle.

Step 2 Pipe line work in a diagonal fashion stacking the lines on top of each other using nozzle nos. 3, 2, 1 across the top of the shell. It is important to pipe all of the lines at the same angle to achieve the desired effect of this border.

Step 3 A simple blossom will add colour to this border.

Step 4 Using a small butterfly is always a popular choice for finishing a border.

Step 5 The addition of a small autumn leaf will give this border a masculine feel.

Ceri's comments

“This border will be a challenge for those who have any sort of dexterity issues as you will have to start piping a line on one side of the shell and finish by tucking it under the other side of the shell, at the same time matching the angle of the previously piped line. All I can say is practice makes perfect, try practicing on a dummy cake or around the edge of a container before attempting this on a real cake.”

Infinity

Step 1 Divide the edge of your cake up into even measurements and then pipe pairs of shells using a no. 13 nozzle. Use a damp paintbrush to touch down any peaks on the tails of your shells as this will ensure your line work will lie evenly.

Step 2 Using a no. 3 nozzle pipe a figure eight in one motion starting in the centre between the two shells and ending in the same place. You will need to use your damp paintbrush to tidy up the centre join.

Step 3 Once the no. 3 piping is completed finish the border with stacked line work using nozzle nos. 2, and 1. This will give a clean open looking border.

Step 4 The unadorned border looks clean and crisp, however adding small embellishments can change the look instantly. Small flowers and leaves are shown here, but baby booties, footballs, wedding bells, butterflies and many more things would work equally as well.

Step 5 Here I have shown a twist to the infinity design, instead of piping a figure eight I have curled the end of my piped line around the head of one of the shells, a completely different look but still the same simplicity.

Ceri's comments

“What could be simpler than mirrored shells and a looping line? When creating this border you will have to measure the circumference of your cake and divide it into equal divisions because it is important that you end with an even number of mirrored shells for this design to work.”

Shell and swirl

Step 1 Divide the edge of your cake up into even measurements and then pipe pairs of shells using a no. 13 nozzle, leaving a space between the pairs that is equal to the length of one shell.

Step 2 Holding your no. 13 nozzle vertically over the space between the pair of shells, pipe a bulb. Use a damp paintbrush to touch down any peak as this will ensure your line work lies smoothly.

Step 3 Pipe a spiral using a no. 44 nozzle. Staying in contact with the bulb beneath will establish a good base for your line work. Once the spiral is complete finish the border with stacked line work using nozzle nos. 3, 2, and 1.

Step 4 This is a dainty border and can also be piped with smaller nozzles to achieve an even more delicate finish. The secret to this border is to make sure each swirl is identical.

Step 5 Simplicity is the key word for this border, keep everything small when you embellish this border or you will overpower it.

Ceri's comments

“This is another favourite of mine, as it's very simple to pipe and lends itself well to the addition of sugar embellishments. This border can work on any sized cake and as either the top or bottom border. It is important to note that dividing the circumference of your cake into equal divisions is essential if all elements of this border are to be evenly spaced.”

Opulent

Step 1 Divide the edge of your cake up into even divisions and then using a no. 44 nozzle pipe three small shells as shown above. These shells should be in the middle of your division and should be piped onto the top surface of the cake.

Step 2 Pipe a larger shell either side of the three small shells using a no. 13 nozzle, making sure you stay within your markings. These shells are piped onto the side of your cake meeting the smaller shells at the edge of the cake.

Step 3 Using a no. 3 nozzle pipe mirrored C shapes onto the larger shells; you will need to use a damp paintbrush to tidy up the ends of your piped lines. Once the no. 3 piping is complete finish the border with stacked line work using nozzle nos. 2 and 1.

Step 4 I completed this border with a small silver ball (dragee) but any small sugar accent could have been added. Be aware if you use a small metallic dragee, over time the royal icing will blacken it. This border works equally as well as a top border when piped upside-down and then mirrored by the bottom border the right way up. The key to the visual effect of this border is accuracy of spacing and neatness of line work.

Ceri's comments

“Whenever I do a cake with no top border this is the border I normally choose. Because of its stylish finish, having this as a bottom border with nothing else on the cake gives an almost art deco feel to the cake. This design can be inverted for a top border or adjusted slightly by piping the three smaller shells onto the top surface of the cake and the two larger shells onto the side of the cake.”

Herringbone shells

Step 1 Pipe shells using a no. 13 nozzle in a herringbone fashion on the upper edge of a cake, one shell will be on the top surface whilst the next will be on the side of the cake.

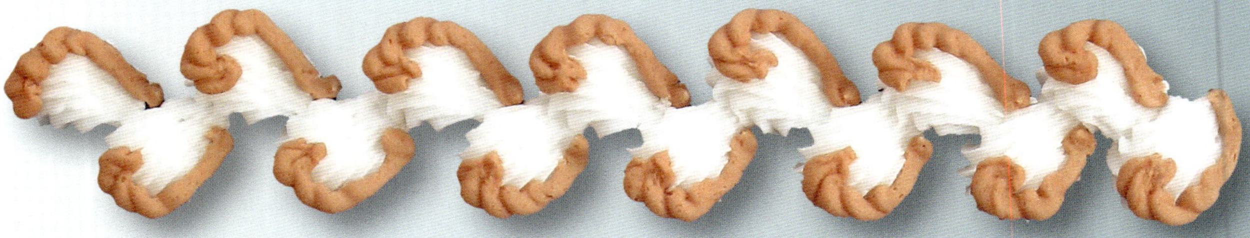

Step 2 Pipe mirrored C scrolls with a no. 3 nozzle onto the shells.

Step 3 Pipe line work stacking the lines on top of each other using nozzle nos. 3, 2, 1.

Step 4 In the image above the border has been piped flat, however on a cake it will give the edges a dimensional finish.

Step 5 A miniature butterfly, tiny blossom or similar embellishment will add the wow factor to this border.

Question mark shells

Step 1 Pipe shells using a no. 13 nozzle. The first shell is piped onto the very edge of the cake; the second shell is piped onto the side of the cake; the last shell is piped onto the top surface of the cake.

Step 2 Pipe the C scrolls with a no. 3 nozzle.

Step 3 Pipe line work stacking the lines on top of each other using nozzle nos. 3, 2, 1.

Step 4 In the image above the border has been piped flat, however on a cake it will give the edges a dimensional finish.

Step 5 I have used simple stars in my design however a small row of coloured dots will add a delicate touch to this design.

Simple scoops

Step 1 Pipe large shells using a no. 13 nozzle; this is achieved by increasing the pressure as you pipe, letting the shell expand before you create the tail.

Step 2 Pipe an even scoop with a no. 44 nozzle onto the bottom third of each large shell. It is very important that all of the scoops are level therefore use a damp paintbrush to nudge them into alignment if needed. Leave the shells and scoops to dry for several hours before moving onto the next step, the weight of the additional line work could pull the scoops out of alignment if they are not dry.

Step 3 Once the shells and scoops have had time to harden, finish the border with stacked line work using nozzle nos. 3, 2, and 1.

Step 4 This is a simple but effective border and can be achieved with any size nozzle appropriate to the design of the cake.

Ceri's comments

"This border is based upon a foundation of a larger shell which means it is best used for larger cake designs. You will also have to wait until the larger shells have dried or crusted before adding any other lines of piping because gravity could pull the shells from the top edge of your cake. This design can also be used as a bottom border or downsized by using smaller piping tips for smaller cake or cookie projects."

Lazy S

Step 1 Pipe large shells using a no. 13 nozzle; this is achieved by increasing the pressure as you pipe, letting the shell expand before you create the tail.

Step 2 Pipe a single S scroll with a no. 3 nozzle starting on the head of one shell and ending at the tail of the next.

Step 3 Over-pipe the S scroll using a no. 3 nozzle. Staying in contact with the scroll beneath will establish a good base for your line work. Once the over piping is completed finish the scroll with stacked line work using nozzle nos. 3, 2, and 1.

Step 4 This is a very sleek looking border but a risky one to pipe. It is best to leave the shells to dry completely before moving onto step 2. Then pipe the S scroll and the over-pipe, and leave that for a further few hours before moving onto the stacked line work. This will prevent the lines sagging as there is very little support for them until they are dry.

Ceri's comments

"This clean and simple border works best on a cake with a continuous edge, no corners, and can be used as either the top or bottom border of a cake. If you wish to make this a quicker more commercial border then you could finish the border at step 2 and still have a beautiful sweeping design."

Rolling wave scrolls

Step 1 Pipe shells using a no. 13 nozzle.

Step 2 Pipe an S scroll over two shells using a no. 44 nozzle.

Step 3 Over-pipe the S scroll using a no. 44 nozzle, staying in contact with the scroll beneath as this will establish a base for your line work.

Step 4 Pipe line work stacking the lines on top of each other using nozzle nos. 3, 2, 1.

Step 5 This border is ideal for use on cakes with a nautical theme due to the wave design.

Ceri's comments

“This is very similar to the Interlocking S Scroll, however because it is piped upon a shell instead of a barrel the look is very neat and compact. This works great for cakes with a continual edge (no corners) and will work for any sized cake. Try experimenting with different sized piping tips because this border looks wonderful if scaled up or down in size.”

The joker

Step 1 Pipe large shells using a no. 13 nozzle; this is achieved by increasing the pressure as you pipe, letting the shell expand before you create the tail. This border is usually piped around the top outer edge of a cake with the shells actually attached to the side of the cake but it can also be piped on the top surface of a cake with the tails pointing towards the centre. When piping this border onto the bottom edge of a cake it is natural to have the tails pointing upwards, an exact opposite to the top edge.

Step 2 Using a no. 3 nozzle pipe a question mark in one motion starting in the centre of the shell and ending at the tip of the tail, you may need to use a damp paintbrush to tidy up the end of your line. Once the no. 3 piping is completed finish the border with stacked line work using nozzle nos. 2 and 1.

Step 3 The visual impact of this border is best achieved if all of the question marks are the same level. To make sure all of the ends of the question marks are even use a strip of paper wrapped around your cake as a guide, if you are doing them on the top surface of a cake then a paper template is useful. Aligning the start of each question mark is a little more difficult as it has to be done visually.

Ceri's comments

“A very easy border to pipe but make sure you have a template which dictates the ends of your shells because unless they are lined up they will not give you the desired effect. I have shown the border here as if it was being used as a top border, however if it is to be used as a bottom border then the design will need to be flipped the other way up.”

Sweeping C on a shell

Step 1 Pipe shells using a no. 13 nozzle, this border is normally piped around the base of a tier and not the top edge.

Step 2 Pipe line work stacking the lines on top of each other using nozzle nos. 3, 2, 1.

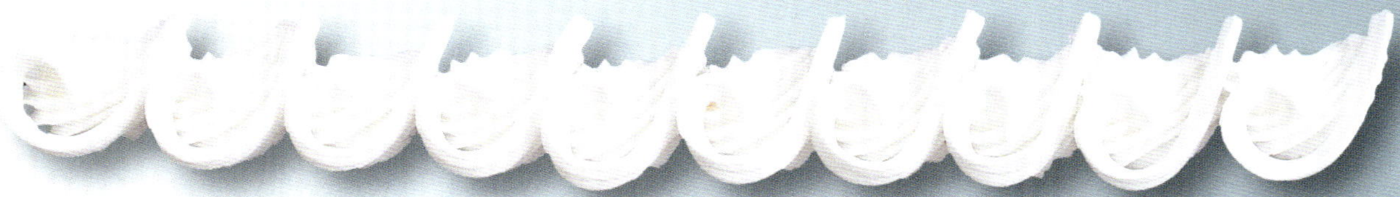

Step 3 This is how the border appears with no embellishment.

Step 4 This is how the border appears with the addition of a simple piped lace off-piece.

Step 5 Using a small butterfly is always a popular choice when looking for finishing touches to a border.

Ceri's comments

“Don't be deceived by the simplicity of this border, each shell needs to be piped at the same angle and then the over-piped line also needs to be on exactly the same angle as its neighbours. With a little practice and planning this is a beautifully understated border, it works well as a bottom border, however if I was using it as a top border I would pipe it directly onto the top surface of the cake, sweeping from the outer edge, inwards toward the centre of the cake.”

Shell and line

Step 1 Pipe shells using a no. 13 nozzle. This border is normally piped around the base of a tier and not the top edge.

Step 2 Pipe the overlapping lines with a no. 1 nozzle.

Step 3 Pipe the second set of overlapping lines with a no. 1 nozzle.

Step 4 This is how the border appears with just the first line of piping and a small embellishment.

Step 5 This is how the same border appears with both lines of piping and a small embellishment. Traditionally this border would have an embellishment to conceal the join of the lines but the embellishment could be as simple as a piped dot.

Ceri's comments

"When I worked in the bakery producing wedding cakes, this was the most requested bottom border. Variations of this can be done as a top border, however it is difficult to get the same delicate effect when positioned as a top edge design. Whenever you create this border it is essential that you create a template for the side of your cake to determine the top line of the shells, if the finished border does not have a straight top edge it will be very obvious."

Hearts in a row

Step 1 Pipe shells using a no. 13 nozzle, this border is normally piped around the top outer edge of a tier, but can also be piped on the top of a cake pointing towards the centre of the cake as in the numbers on a clock.

Step 2 Pipe a pair of small mirrored C scrolls with a no. 3 nozzle to establish the heart shape.

Step 3 Pipe line work stacking the lines on top of each other using nozzle nos. 3, 2, 1.

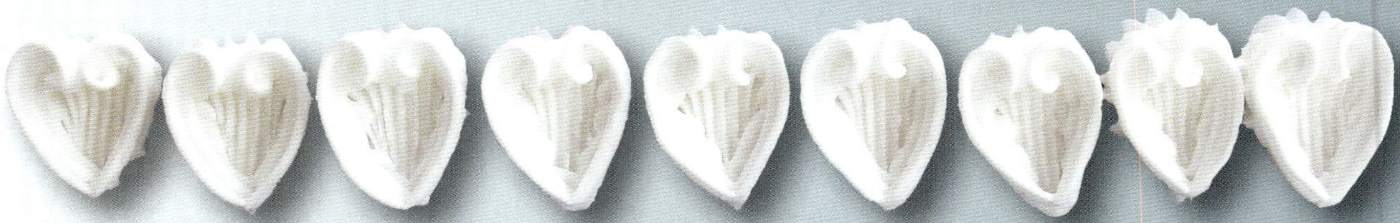

Step 4 This is how the finished border appears.

Step 5 A simple coloured blossom and leaf can add the wow factor to your finished cake, as shown here.

Ceri's comments

“If you are using the Shell and Line border as a bottom border, then this is the perfect complimentary top border, again the secret to this border is repetition of shape. This border can be used as a bottom border, however it is best to invert it so that the hearts point upwards. If you are apprehensive about piping this, then the complete individual shells can be piped onto a piece of wax paper or a piece of cellophane (lightly smeared with white vegetable fat), once dried they can then be stuck onto the side of the cake.”

Three in a row

Step 1 Pipe a single line with a no. 13 nozzle. If you are piping around the top edge of the cake this is best achieved with a tilting turntable. Don't worry if the line is not completed in one action, just make sure the joins are smoothed out with a damp paintbrush. It is best to leave the line to dry completely before moving onto the following steps.

Step 2 Pipe a row of shells, as shown, above the line using a no. 13 nozzle, spacing them evenly.

Step 3 Pipe a row of shells, as shown, below the line using a no. 13 nozzle, making sure you match the spacing with the shells above the line.

Step 4 Pipe a row of shells on top of the line using a no. 13 nozzle, making sure you match the spacing with the other shells.

Step 5 This is a simple border and works as a triple shell on the top edge of a cake, however if you wish to do this around the base of your cake do not pipe the shells in step 2, leave it as two rows of shells only. If you try to make it three rows your shells will look squashed. To give variety to this border, pipe one of the rows of shells in a complimentary colour to your overall design.

Single S scroll

Step 1 Barrels piped with a no. 44 nozzle. Be aware that if you are doing an S scroll over two barrels you must pipe an even number of barrels on your cake.

Step 2 Pipe an S scroll using a no. 44 nozzle.

Step 3 Over-pipe the S scroll using a no. 44 nozzle, staying in contact with the scroll beneath as this will establish a base for your line work.

Step 4 Pipe line work stacking the lines on top of each other using nozzle nos. 3, 2, 1.

Step 5 This is how your completed border should appear; this border lends itself to simple elegant lines in a design.

Ceri's comments

"This is one of the first piped scrolls any student would learn, mastering its shape and form will enable you to create many other borders as this shape is a key element of English Over-piping. If used as a stand alone piped piece, it can be piped as a top or bottom border, it can even be inverted."

Double S scroll

Step 1 Barrels piped with a no. 44 nozzle. Be aware that if you are doing a double S scroll over two barrels you must pipe an even number of barrels on your cake.

Step 2 Pipe a double S scroll using a no. 44 nozzle.

Step 3 Over-pipe the S scrolls using a no. 44 nozzle, staying in contact with the scroll beneath as this will establish a base for your line work. If possible, have the tails of the scrolls joining at the tip.

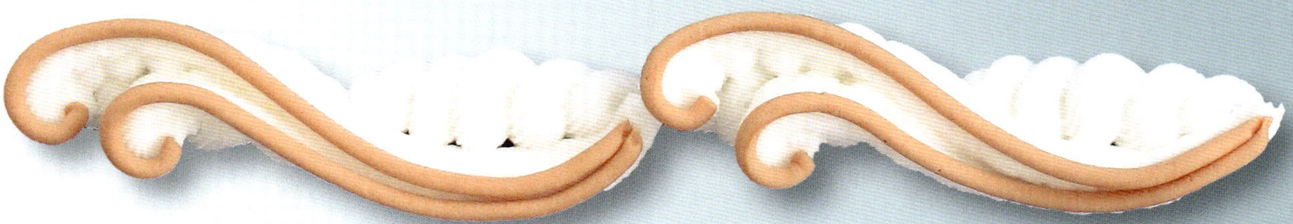

Step 4 Pipe line work stacking the lines on top of each other using nozzle nos. 3, 2, 1.

Step 5 This is how your completed border should appear; this border lends itself to simple elegant lines in a design.

Ceri's comments

“A good example of developing a single element to create a new border, this can be piped in many different ways and directions. It gives a very classical look to any cake it adorns. The texture and the overall shape of this border will alter if you change the size of the piping tips.”

Interlocking S scroll

Step 1 Barrels piped with a no. 44 nozzle.

Step 2 Pipe an S scroll using a no. 44 nozzle.

Step 3 Over-pipe the S scroll using a no. 44 nozzle, staying in contact with the scroll beneath as this will establish a base for your line work.

Step 4 Pipe line work stacking the lines on top of each other using nozzle nos. 3, 2, 1.

Step 5 This is how your completed border should appear; this border lends itself to simple elegant lines in a design and is often used for masculine cakes.

Ceri's comments

"This is possibly one of my favourite borders, it's so versatile allowing decorative elements to be placed within its sweeping shapes. This border works best on a cake with a continual edge – a cake with corners will cause you design problems as it's meant to be a sweeping continual design. A great border for a masculine cake, think of rolling waves, rope or chain links."

S and C scroll

Step 1 Barrels piped with a no. 44 nozzle. Be aware that if you are doing an S and C scroll over two barrels you must pipe an even number of barrels on your cake.

Step 2 Pipe an S and C scroll using a no. 44 nozzle.

Step 3 Over-pipe the S and C scrolls using a no. 44 nozzle, staying in contact with the scrolls beneath as this will establish a base for your line work. If possible, have the tails of the scrolls joining at the tip.

Step 4 Pipe line work stacking the lines on top of each other using nozzle nos. 3, 2, 1.

Step 5 This is how your completed border should appear; this border lends itself to larger cakes due to the elaborate nature of the border.

Ceri's comments

“When anyone talks about English Over-piping the first border they think of is this. Indicative of the sweeping lines found within historical English decor, think of heraldic shields, silverware designs, and manor house ceiling mouldings and you will find these shapes. A very versatile border which will work for both top and bottom borders and lend itself to any shaped cake.”

Double S and C scroll

Step 1 Barrels piped with a no. 13 nozzle.

Step 2 Pipe a double S and C scroll using a no. 44 nozzle.

Step 3 Over-pipe the double S and C scroll using a no. 44 nozzle, staying in contact with the scrolls beneath as this will establish a base for your line work. If possible, have the tails of the scrolls joining at the tip.

Step 4 Pipe line work stacking the lines on top of each other using nozzle nos. 3, 2, 1.

Step 5 This is how your completed border should appear; this border can appear very elaborate and will over-power a smaller cake.

S and cresting C scroll

Step 1 Barrels piped with a no. 13 nozzle.

Step 2 Pipe an S and cresting C scroll using a no. 44 nozzle.

Step 3 Over-pipe the S and cresting C scrolls using a no. 44 nozzle, staying in contact with the scrolls beneath as this will establish a base for your line work. If possible, have the tails of the scrolls joining at the tip.

Step 4 Pipe line work stacking the lines on top of each other using nozzle nos. 3, 2, 1.

Step 5 This is how your completed border should appear; this border lends itself to larger cakes due to the elaborate nature of the border.

Ceri's comments

"When you are used to piping S and C Scrolls you will find this border a little bit of a challenge as piping a cresting C Scroll behind an S Scroll will not feel natural. The whole border will have a very open appearance and works best on larger cakes. It can be used as either a top or bottom border."

S and hanging C scroll

Step 1 Barrels piped with a no. 13 nozzle.

Step 2 Pipe an S and hanging C scroll using a no. 44 nozzle.

Step 3 Over-pipe the S and hanging C scrolls using a no. 44 nozzle, staying in contact with the scrolls beneath as this will establish a base for your line work. If possible, have the tails of the scrolls joining at the tip.

Step 4 Pipe line work stacking the lines on top of each other using nozzle nos. 3, 2, 1.

Step 5 This is how your completed border should appear; this border lends itself to larger cakes due to the elaborate nature of the border.

Coach and horses

Step 1 The barrels are piped with a no. 44 nozzle. Your cake will require an even number of barrels to complete this border.

Step 2 Pipe an S scroll with a no. 44 nozzle over two barrels and then continue to pipe two cresting C's on the second barrel.

Step 3 Over-pipe the S scroll and cresting C scrolls using a no. 44 nozzle. Staying in contact with the scrolls beneath will establish a good base for your line work. Once the over piping is completed finish the border with stacked line work using nozzle nos. 3, 2, and 1.

Step 4 This border works best on cakes which are either round or oval. If you wish to do this design on a cake which has corners a very pleasant effect can be achieved by piping every other set of scrolls in the opposite direction. This will result in a classic corner design where either the heads or tails meet, a perfect place to add a small design element. I always recommend sketching your design before piping to obtain the best effects.

Ceri's comments

"The length and complexity of this border is best displayed upon large cakes, however it is very versatile as it will work on any shape and can be piped as both a top or bottom border, it can even be piped as a mirrored design."

Dainty valentines

Step 1 The barrels are piped with a no. 44 nozzle, your cake will require three barrels to complete each sequence of this border.

Step 2 Firstly pipe the S scrolls over the end barrels with a no. 44 nozzle and then continue to pipe two C's scrolls onto the centre barrel. Take care to mirror the shapes of the scrolls, if they are slightly out of line use a damp paintbrush to nudge them into place.

Step 3 Over-pipe the S and C scrolls using a no. 44 nozzle. Staying in contact with the scrolls beneath will establish a good base for your line work. Once the over piping is completed finish the border with stacked line work using nozzle nos. 3, 2, and 1.

Step 4 This border is designed for the larger cake and is best suited to cakes with corners such as squares, octagons, pentagons, etc. If used on a tiered cake make sure that the design will fit onto the top or smallest tier without it appearing squashed before proceeding. The C scrolls in this design are the perfect framework for a small design element, as shown here.

Ceri's comments

"This border is definitely best used on cakes with straight edges, square cakes will give you the most pleasing results. I have used this once or twice on round cakes but the overall impact of the design is lost as the border curves around the cake."

Elegance

Step 1 Barrels piped with a no. 13 nozzle. Be aware that if you are doing this border over two barrels you must pipe an even number of barrels on your cake.

Step 2 Pipe an S, double C and a reverse hanging C scroll using a no. 44 nozzle.

Step 3 Over-pipe all of the scrolls using a no. 44 nozzle, staying in contact with the scrolls beneath as this will establish a base for your line work. If possible, have the tails of the scrolls joining at the tip.

Step 4 Pipe line work stacking the lines on top of each other using nozzle nos. 3, 2, 1.

Step 5 This is a very beautiful border which should only be piped onto a large cake. If it is piped onto a tiered cake then I recommend reducing the nozzle sizes for the barrels and scrolls on each tier, reducing the overall impact of the border the higher up the tiers you progress.

Scroll and line

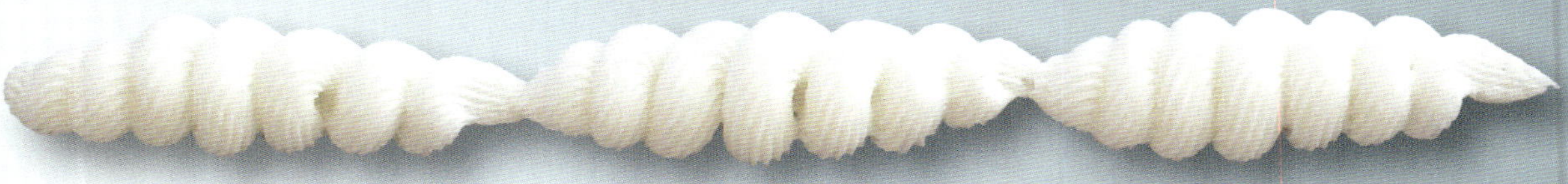

Step 1 The barrels are piped with a no. 44 nozzle; be aware that there needs to be an even number of barrels on your cake as every other section of scroll work is inverted.

Step 2 Pipe an S and C scroll using a no. 44 nozzle onto each barrel, remembering that every other S and C scroll needs to be inverted.

Step 3 Over-pipe the S and C scrolls using a no. 44 nozzle. Staying in contact with the scroll beneath will establish a good base for your line work. Once the over piping is complete finish the scrolls with stacked line work using nozzle nos. 3, 2, and 1.

Step 4 Once your stacked line work is completely dry, pipe the first line between each scroll using a no. 1 nozzle. By doing this you will be able to visually check if your angles are evenly matched. Once this has been achieved continue to pipe lines between your S and C scrolls, staying parallel to your first line. This alignment will naturally change as you curve towards the tapered ends of your scrolls. A damp paintbrush is essential to keep your line ends tidy.

Step 5 This is possibly my favourite border as it needs no adornment and achieves the wow factor by the sheer nature of its delicate bridging lines. This also works well with the lines in a complimentary colour to your cake design.

Cresting C scrolls

Step 1 Barrels piped with a no. 44 nozzle.

Step 2 Pipe a C scroll using a no. 44 nozzle.

Step 3 Over-pipe the C scroll using a no. 44 nozzle, staying in contact with the scroll beneath as this will establish a base for your line work.

Step 4 Pipe line work stacking the lines on top of each other using nozzle nos. 3, 2, 1.

Step 5 This is how your completed border should appear and is shown here with simple peak-a-boo blossoms nestling in the curve of the C.

Ceri's comments

"Very versatile in its application, the Cresting C Scroll can be used on any shaped cake and on either of the cake edges. The shape of this border is elegant in itself, however it lends itself to the addition of sugar pieces, such as flowers, butterflies, leaves, etc."

C scroll

Step 1 Barrels piped with a no. 44 nozzle.

Step 2 Pipe a C scroll using a no. 44 nozzle.

Step 3 Over-pipe the C scroll using a no. 44 nozzle, staying in contact with the scroll beneath as this will establish a base for your line work.

Step 4 Pipe line work stacking the lines on top of each other using nozzle nos. 3, 2, 1.

Step 5 This is how your completed border should appear and is shown here with simple blossoms nestling in the curve of the C, however any small embellishment could be used.

Ceri's comments

“This quick little border may seem simple, but the secret to its appearance is accuracy. Always make sure you measure the circumference of your cake and mark the equal divisions before piping your barrels to enable you to get equal repetition of design. This border works on any shaped cake and can be piped in many different ways, this is one to experiment with.”

Bookend C scrolls

Step 1 Pipe a barrel using a no. 13 nozzle.

Step 2 Pipe mirrored C scrolls using a no. 44 nozzle.

Step 3 Over-pipe the C scroll using a no. 44 nozzle, staying in contact with the scroll beneath as this will establish a base for your line work.

Step 4 Pipe line work stacking the lines on top of each other using nozzle nos. 3, 2, 1.

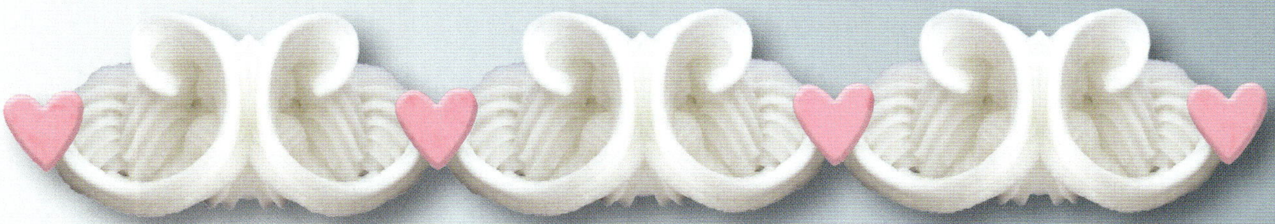

Step 5 This finished border will appear very elaborate once on a cake and can overpower a smaller design.

Ceri's comments

"This will give you a very ornate, almost frilled look to your cake. It suits both the top and bottom edges of the cake, but can appear heavy on smaller cakes. Symmetry is the secret to this balanced design so make sure you have a slightly damp paintbrush with you when you pipe this border because you can slightly adjust the shape of a piped line whilst it is still wet."

C scoops

Step 1 Pipe a barrel using a no. 13 nozzle.

Step 2 Pipe a double-ended C scroll or scoop using a no. 44 nozzle.

Step 3 Over-pipe the C scroll using a no. 44 nozzle, staying in contact with the scroll beneath as this will establish a base for your line work.

Step 4 Pipe line work stacking the lines on top of each other using nozzle nos. 3, 2, 1.

Step 5 This finished border is elegant on its own, however it is perfect for small embellishments or garlands of blossoms.

Ceri's comments

"The C scoop is often used as a decorative element within other borders and lends itself to the larger cake designs as it can appear heavy on smaller cakes. The biggest challenge you will have when piping this border is symmetry. It is also wise to be aware of gravity if used as a top border – let the barrel dry before building upon it as the overall weight of the royal icing may distort the scoops shape."

Swags

Step 1 Pipe a barrel using a no. 13 nozzle.

Step 2 Pipe a rope using a no. 44 nozzle underneath the barrel and then another rope above it on the curve of the barrel.

Step 3 Pipe a line under the first rope using a no. 44 nozzle, then over-pipe the two ropes using a no. 44 nozzle, staying in contact with the rope as this will establish a base for your line work.

Step 4 Pipe line work stacking the lines on top of each other using nozzle nos. 3, 2, 1 on top of each of the piped lines.

Step 5 This is a very heavy border therefore I recommend piping your barrels first and leaving them to completely dry before piping the ropes and line work.

Mirrored scoops

Step 1 Pipe a barrel using a no. 13 nozzle.

Step 2 Pipe a rope either side of the barrel using a no. 44 nozzle to form the scoops.

Step 3 Over-pipe the ropes using a no. 44 nozzle, staying in contact with the rope beneath as this will establish a base for your line work.

Step 4 Pipe line work stacking the lines on top of each other using nozzle nos. 3, 2, 1.

Step 5 This finished border is elegant on its own, however it is also perfect for small embellishments due to its picture frame nature.

Scoop and heart

Step 1 Pipe the pairs of shells and the barrels using a no. 13 nozzle ensuring to space them evenly around your cake.

Step 2 Pipe mirrored C's onto the shells and a rope onto the barrel using a no. 44 nozzle.

Step 3 Over-pipe the rope using a no. 44 nozzle, staying in contact with the rope beneath as this will establish a good base for your line work.

Step 4 Pipe line work stacking the lines on top of each other using nozzle nos. 3, 2, 1 on top of each of the piped lines.

Step 5 This border is best suited to larger cakes, however by using smaller nozzles this will give you a very delicate finish on a smaller cake.

Sports car

Step 1 The barrels and shells are both piped with a no. 13 nozzle. It is a border over one barrel, therefore mark the circumference of your cake into even divisions of your choice. Pipe one barrel and shell before moving onto the next barrel, that way you will not damage the second barrel when fitting in the first shell.

Step 2 Pipe a single S scroll with a no. 44 nozzle over one barrel.

Step 3 Over-pipe the S scroll using a no. 44 nozzle. Staying in contact with the scroll beneath will establish a good base for your line work. Once the over piping is completed finish the scroll with stacked line work using nozzle nos. 3, 2, and 1.

Step 4 Using a no. 3 nozzle pipe a spiral onto the shell starting where the shell meets the scroll, you will need to use a damp paintbrush to tidy up the ends of your piped line. Once the no. 3 piping is completed finish the spiral with stacked line work using nozzle nos. 2 and 1.

Step 5 This border visually flows around a cake and is very versatile as every other scroll could be reversed to give you an entirely different look.

Daisy Daisy

Step 1 Divide the edge of your cake up into even measurements and then pipe the S shapes using a no. 13 nozzle. Use a damp paintbrush to touch down any peaks at the ends of your piping as this will ensure your line work will lie evenly.

Step 2 Finish the border with stacked line work using nozzle nos. 3, 2, and 1.

Step 3 This is a simple border to achieve but the secret to its impact is even spacing and neat piping. To give a slightly different effect try piping each S in the opposite direction, your curls will then be mirrored.

Step 4 This border is best piped onto a curved surface so it is perfect for use on a sugarpaste coated cake. If you choose to pipe this onto a royal icing coated cake then you will need to decide if the border sits on the top surface or the side of your cake. The S shape could be piped onto a barrel if desired, this would then work on a cake with a sharp edge. Just the addition of a piped daisy or sugar element can change a simple border like this into an eye catching design element.

Ceri's comments

"Because of its sweeping nature, this border will not work on a cake with a sharp top edge and it's nearly impossible to pipe it as a bottom border to a cake. This Daisy Daisy border is best piped onto a flat surface so it could be piped onto the surface of your cake board as an edge design or directly onto the top surface of a cake."

Rope and blade

Step 1 Pipe an even rope using a no. 13 nozzle. This border is normally piped around the top edge of a cake.

Step 2 Pipe a smaller rope into the creases in the larger rope using a no. 3 nozzle.

Step 3 Over-pipe the smaller ropes by piping line work, stacking the lines on top of each other using nozzle nos. 3, 2, 1.

Step 4 The secret to this border is precision in piping and can be difficult to execute as you will be piping from the top surface to the side surface of the cake.

Step 5 This is a very clean looking border which is perfect for small embellishments such as tiny leaves.

Flower basket scroll

Step 1 Pipe an even rope around your cake using a no. 13 nozzle. As shown here, an evenly piped rope can be a good border in itself if piped well.

Step 2 At this point you need to mark your rope into equal portions, this is a long border and takes the space of approximately three average barrels. Pipe a single S scroll with a no. 44 nozzle over two thirds of your allotted space and then pipe another S scroll in the opposite direction inverted, as shown above. It is best to practice this technique before attempting it on a cake to perfect the required curves.

Step 3 Over-pipe the S scrolls using a no. 44 nozzle. Staying in contact with the scrolls beneath will establish a good base for your line work. If time allows leave your border to dry a little before moving on. Once the over piping is completed and dry, finish the border with stacked line work using nozzle nos. 3, 2, and 1.

Step 4 As you pipe this border the basket area will appear to be bigger than required, this is an illusion. As soon as you fill the basket area with flowers it will regain its proportions. This border is perfect for larger cakes and works wonderfully if used on a cake with corners where this border can occupy an entire side panel of a cake. When used on a tiered wedding cake each border will look proportionately correct with the reduction of each tier size.

Double S and triple C

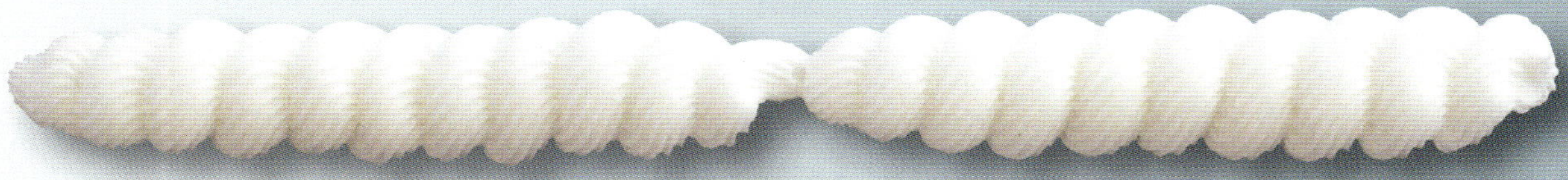

Step 1 The barrels are piped with a no. 44 nozzle, your cake will require an even number of barrels to complete this border.

Step 2 Pipe a double S scroll with a no. 44 nozzle over one barrel and then continue to pipe three C scrolls on the second barrel.

Step 3 Over-pipe the S and C scrolls using a no. 44 nozzle. Staying in contact with the scrolls beneath will establish a good base for your line work. Once the over piping is complete, finish the border with stacked line work using nozzle nos. 3, 2, and 1.

Step 4 This border works best on cakes which are either round or oval. If you wish to do this design on a cake which has corners a very pleasant effect can be achieved by piping every other set of the border in the opposite direction. This will result in a classic corner design where either the heads or tails meet, a perfect place to add a small design element. I always recommend sketching your design before piping to obtain the best effects.

Ceri's comments

“This is a very large border and works best on cakes that are both larger and taller because by its very nature this border fills space. If you add this as a top and bottom border to a shallow cake you will not have much space on the side of your cake for any further embellishments and the cake will look very heavy and squat.”

Lambeth style 1

Step 1 Pipe large shells using a no. 13 nozzle. It is very important to note that you need to leave enough space between the shells to complete the rest of the piped border.

Step 2 Pipe a C scroll wrapped around the head of the shell using a no. 3 nozzle, paying particular attention to where on the shell you start to pipe and match all other C scrolls to it for uniformity.

Step 3 Pipe a single S scroll with a no. 44 nozzle starting on top of one shell and wrapping around the next, paying particular attention to where on the shell you start and match all other S scrolls to it.

Step 4 Over-pipe the S scrolls only using a no. 44 nozzle. Staying in contact with the scroll beneath will establish a good base for your line work. Once the over piping is complete finish the S scrolls with stacked line work using nozzle nos. 3, 2, and 1.

Step 5 The secret to high impact borders such as this is accuracy of piping. This is more easily achieved when piping onto a cake so if you first practice on a board do not be disheartened. The joy of this Lambeth style border is you could stop at any of the steps and still have an impressive border on your cake.

Lambeth style 2

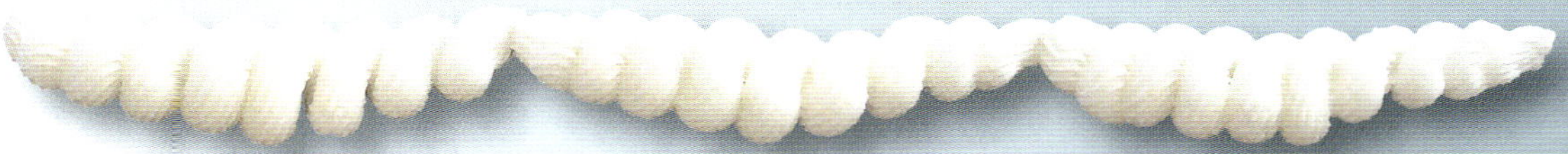

Step 1 The barrels are piped with a no. 44 nozzle, these should be piped onto the side of your cake and not onto the top edge as normal.

Step 2 Pipe pairs of shells with a no. 13 nozzle, as shown above. These shells should be piped onto the top surface of the cake and meet the barrel at the edge of your cake.

Step 3 Using a no. 3 nozzle pipe mirrored C shapes onto the shells; you will need to use a damp paintbrush to tidy up the ends of your piped lines. Once the no. 3 piping is complete finish the shells with stacked line work using nozzle nos 2 and 1.

Step 4 Pipe a double line under each barrel using a no. 44 nozzle. It is wise to leave these to dry for a couple of hours before finishing them with stacked line work using nozzle nos. 3, 2, and 1 as they may sag.

Step 5 This border is perfect for the addition of sugar design elements such as butterflies, as shown here. However, the area where all the lines meet is also perfect for piped doves, small sugar bells or a tiny bow, the options are endless.

Lambeth style 3

Step 1 Pipe large shells using a no. 13 nozzle; this is achieved by increasing the pressure as you pipe, letting the shell expand before you create the tail. This border is usually piped around the top outer edge of a cake with the shells actually attached to the side of the cake, but it can also be piped on the top surface of a cake with the tails pointing towards the centre. When piping this border onto the bottom edge of a cake it is natural to have the tails pointing upwards, an exact opposite to the image above.

Step 2 Using a no. 44 nozzle, pipe a line starting at the head of the shell and ending at its tail, then continue to pipe a small C shape on either side of the central line. Use a damp paintbrush to tidy up the ends of your lines. Next pipe the stacked line work using nozzle nos. 3, 2, and 1 onto the straight central line. Once all of the stacked line work is complete pipe a roped C shape either side of the line work using a no. 3 nozzle.

Step 3 The visual impact of this border is best achieved if all of the line ends are the same level. To make sure all of the ends are even use a strip of paper wrapped around your cake as a guide; if you are doing them on the top surface of a cake then a paper template is useful.

Lambeth style 4

Step 1 Cut a paper strip that fits exactly around your cake. Using a pencil & ruler divide this template into equal divisions. You will need to calculate how many V shapes you require to fit your template perfectly. Cut out the V shapes and then wrap the template around your cake making sure it touches the desired edge. Secure the template to itself with tape so that it does not move. At this stage your cake should look as if it is wrapped in a paper party hat. If you are doing a bottom border then this image would be inverted.

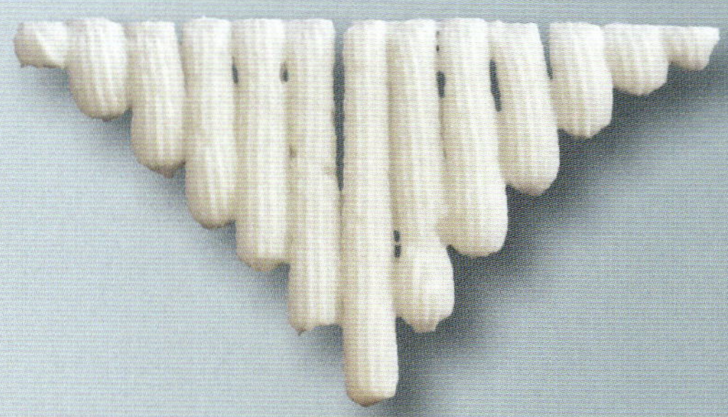

Step 2 Using a no. 44 nozzle pipe vertical lines filling in the spaces in your template, this is best achieved by using a tilting turntable or raising one edge of your cake board on a wedge. Each space should have exactly the same number of lines and cleaning the end of your nozzle between each line will ensure sharp ends to these piped lines. Once these lines are finished pipe another line with a no. 3 nozzle into the valley between the previous lines. Once all of these lines are complete, pipe a large barrel with a no. 13 nozzle above the flat edge of your lines. This will be supported by the top surface of your cake.

Step 3 Pipe a long inverted scoop over the top of the barrel, as shown above. It is wise to leave these scoops for a couple of hours to dry before finishing them with stacked line work using nozzle nos. 3, 2, and 1 as they may sag.

Step 4 This is a very impressive border however it only works well on a larger cake as it seems to overpower a small cake. This border is great in colour and you could easily stop at step 2 and have a striking border with the chance to add colour to your design. For another variation of this border invert the scoop. When used as a bottom border the entire design is inverted.

Lambeth style 5

Step 1 This border would normally lay on a flat surface therefore it is best piped onto the board around the cake or the top surface of your cake. If piped onto the top surface a paper template in the centre of your cake will aid you in ending all of your curving shells on the same line. The shells are piped with a no. 13 nozzle.

Step 2 Using a no. 44 nozzle pipe a large C shape onto the top of the shell, trying to make each C shape match the previous one. Use a damp paintbrush to nudge them into alignment if necessary.

Step 3 Pipe a small C using a no. 3 nozzle into the lower curve of the larger C shape. There will be no more piping added to this small C shape so take care to tidy its shape up with a damp paintbrush if necessary.

Step 4 Finish the border by piping stacked line work using nozzle nos. 3, 2, and 1 onto the large C shape. To maintain the uniform curve of the C shapes use a damp paintbrush to position the lines if needed.

Step 5 Take care when using this border in your design as it can look heavy on a smaller cake and will have the illusion of closing in the top surface of any cake it is piped upon. If this border is piped onto a top surface then continual line work around its inner edge is the perfect way to compliment this lovely border.

Lambeth style 6

Step 1 This border would normal lay on a flat surface therefore it is best piped onto the board around the cake or the top surface. If piped onto the top surface, a paper template in the centre of your cake will aid you in ending all of your curving shells on the same line. The elongated curving shells are evenly spaced and piped with a no. 13 nozzle; once these are completed, a small and less curving shell is piped with the same nozzle into the valleys between.

Step 2 Using a no. 44 nozzle pipe a large cresting C shape onto the top of the shell making each C shape match the previous one. Use a damp paintbrush to nudge them into alignment, if necessary. Finish the border by piping stacked line work using nozzle nos. 3, 2, and 1 onto the cresting C shape. To maintain the uniform curve of the C shapes use a damp paintbrush to position the lines if needed.

Step 3 Because of the nature of this border you can alter the width of it to suit your overall design. Reducing the size of the nozzles used for the shells will give you a more delicate effect. If this border is piped onto the top surface of a cake then continual line work around its inner edge is the perfect way to compliment this simple border.